Growing Up

written by Ruth Shannon Odor
illustrated by Helen Simon

THE CHILD'S WORLD

ELGIN, ILLINOIS 60120

To the teacher or parent:

This book stresses assuming responsibility for everyday tasks, obeying parents, being thoughtful and kind, helping others. Lori goes through an entire day doing these things. Her parents are proud of her, and God is pleased.

The book may be used to introduce discussion. Here are some questions you may ask. 1. How many helpful things did Lori do? Can you name them? 2. What helpful things can you do at home? 3. What helpful things can you do at school? 4. Do you thank God for food before each meal? Why should we thank God? 5. When did Lori obey her mother even though she didn't want to? 6. Can you think of a time when you didn't want to obey your Mother or Father? 7. What hard jobs do you do all by yourself? 8. How do you feel when you do something hard all by yourself? 9. How do you feel when you help someone? 10. Who else besides your Mother and Father is pleased when you obey and help?

Distributed by Standard Publishing, 8121 Hamilton Avenue, Cincinnati, Ohio 45231.

Library of Congress Cataloging in Publication Data

Odor, Ruth Shannon.
  Growing up.

  (A Values series)
  Published (c1976) under title: Lori's day.
  SUMMARY: A little girl's helpful actions during the day are a sign she is really growing up.
  [1. Responsibility—Fiction.   2. Christian life—Fiction]   I. Simon, Helen.   II. Title. III. Series.
PZ7.0255Gr   [E]   79-11393
ISBN 0-89565-075-4

Growing Up

"Ho-hum," yawned Lori
as she climbed out of bed.
She put on her red jumper
and white blouse.

Lori sat at the table.
She bowed her head.
"Thank You, God, for cereal
and milk," she said.
Then she ate her breakfast.
And Mother went to see
about Lori's baby brother.

Lori picked up the empty bowl
and the glass and the spoon.
She carried them to the sink
and put them on the counter.

Yes, she did.
All by herself.

Just then, Mother came into the kitchen.
"Why, thank you, Lori," she said.
"What a good helper you are.
You're growing up."

Lori ran outside to play.
She climbed on her red tricycle.
She rode it fast
up and down the sidewalk
in front of her house.
Then she rode it slowly
up and down the sidewalk
in front of her house.

Lori saw Mrs. Wilson
coming down the street.
Mrs. Wilson was very old
and always walked
very, very slowly.
Lori parked her tricycle
beside the sidewalk
so that Mrs. Wilson
could get by.

Good morning, Mrs. Wilson," she said.

"Good morning, Lori," said Mrs. Wilson.
"How kind you are! My, you're growing
up."

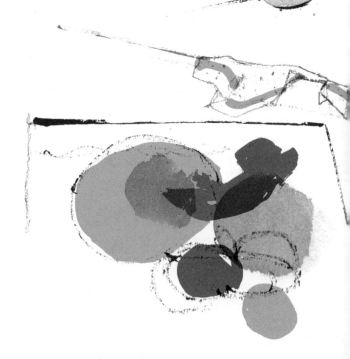

After lunch, Lori's mother said,
"Nap time."

"I don't want to take a nap,"
grumbled Lori.

"Don't argue about it," said her mother.
"You need a nap."

Lori felt like arguing — but —
she went to her room,
took off her shoes,
and climbed into bed.

Yes, she did.
All by herself.

After Lori woke up,
she ran to Mother.
Mother let her hold her baby brother
for a while.
She held him carefully.

Yes, she did.
All by herself.

Lori put on her coat and hat
and played in the back yard
while her Mother got supper.
She heard a car stop in the driveway.
She ran to the front yard.
It was Daddy.
He had his arms full of grocery bags.

Lori ran to the door.
She opened it.
She held it open for Daddy.

Yes, she did.
All by herself.

"Thank you, Lori," said Daddy
as he put the grocery bags
on the kitchen counter.
"What a good helper you are.
You're growing up."

That night, Lori thanked God
for the good day.
Then Mother tucked her
into bed.
"Lori, I'm proud of you,"
she said.
"You're growing up."

"You mean growing taller
and bigger?" asked Lori.

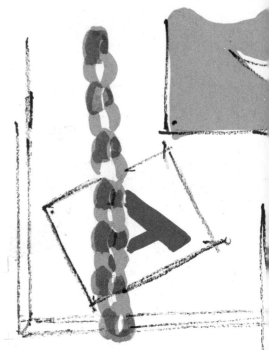

"Yes," said Mother. "But more important, you're learning to obey Mother and Daddy, to help other people, and to do all kinds of things all by yourself. That's just the way God wants you to grow."

"Is He glad?" asked Lori.

"Yes, Lori," said Mother. "Very glad."

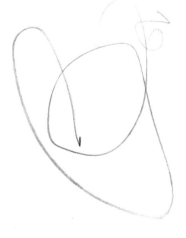